WILDLIFE IN BLOOM SERIES

Little Coyote

BY AUTHOR & CONSERVATIONIST

LINDA BLACKMOOR

ISBN: 978-1-966417-20-0 (PRINT)

PUBLISHED BY QUILL PRESS. LINDA BLACKMOOR'S TITLES MAY BE
PURCHASED IN BULK FOR EDUCATIONAL, BUSINESS, FUNDRAISING, OR
SALES PROMOTIONAL USE. FOR INFORMATION, PLEASE EMAIL
HELLO@LINDABLACKMOOR.COM

FIRST PRINT EDITION: 2025

LINDA BLACKMOOR
WWW.LINDABLACKMOOR.COM

SPECIES

Coyotes are canines belonging to the Canidae family, closely related to wolves and foxes. Their scientific name is Canis latrans, meaning "barking dog," which reflects their wide range of vocalizations. Found only in North and Central America, coyotes thrive in habitats from deserts and plains to forests and even cities. Their success comes from adaptability and a flexible diet that helps them survive.

LOOKS

Coyotes typically weigh between 20 to 50 pounds, with a body length of around 3 to 4 feet, not counting their bushy tail. Their fur is usually grayish-brown with white or cream-colored throats, but coat colors can change by region. They have large ears and slender muzzles, giving them a sleek, alert look. Strong legs and a bushy tail help them balance while running and maneuvering through terrain.

HABITAT

Coyotes flourish in many habitats, including deserts, grasslands, forests, mountains, and even neighborhoods. They dig dens or use abandoned burrows for shelter, where they rest or care for pups. Urban coyotes adapt by hunting rodents, scavenging scraps, and finding cover in parks or under buildings. This remarkable ability to live alongside humans has expanded their range across the continent.

DIET

As omnivores, coyotes have a flexible diet that includes small mammals, birds, insects, fruit, and carrion. They often hunt in pairs, increasing success against larger prey like deer, especially when food is scarce. In cities, coyotes may eat rodents, trash, or pet food left outdoors. This wide-ranging menu helps them adjust to different seasons and habitats.

VOCALS

Coyotes are famous for their vocalizations, using howls, yips, barks, and whines to communicate over long distances. Families gather at night to howl, keeping track of each other's locations and warning rival coyotes away. Body language, like tail and ear positions, adds extra detail to their messages. These signals help them coordinate hunts and maintain strong social bonds.

SOCIAL

Although coyotes often travel alone, they may form family packs—a mated pair and their pups. Sometimes older offspring stay to help raise new litters, increasing pup survival. Packs cooperate in hunting and defending territories, but individuals can also split away to find new areas. This blend of independence and teamwork gives coyotes a unique social dynamic.

BABIES

Coyotes mate in late winter, and after about 63 days, the female gives birth to litters ranging from 4 to 7 pups. Pups are born blind and rely entirely on their mother's milk for the first weeks of life. Both parents bring food and protect the growing pups, teaching them how to hunt. By fall, young coyotes begin to explore on their own, ready to find their own paths.

ADAPT

Coyotes show adaptability by shifting hunting times, altering diets, and adjusting den locations to avoid conflicts. They are mostly nocturnal in urban areas to steer clear of people but can be active during the day in remote regions. Their boldness and keen senses help them thrive where larger predators cannot. This ability to fit into changing environments has allowed their populations to grow.

SPEED

Coyotes can run up to 40 miles per hour (64 kilometers per hour) when chasing prey or escaping danger. Their lean bodies and long legs give them excellent stamina over long distances. They also leap over fences or obstacles with ease, aided by strong hind legs. Quick reflexes and agility let them dodge threats and catch fast-moving prey.

COYOTE FACTS #10

SCAVENGE

In addition to hunting, coyotes are skilled scavengers, taking advantage of carrion left by other predators or roadkills. This scavenging behavior helps them gather food during harsh winters or when prey is scarce. By cleaning up carcasses, they help keep ecosystems tidy and reduce the spread of disease. This opportunistic feeding strategy further supports their success in diverse habitats.

COYOTE FACTS #11

PREDATOR

Adult coyotes have few natural predators, though wolves, mountain lions, and bears may sometimes attack them. Humans pose the greatest threat through hunting, habitat loss, and vehicles. Coyotes avoid stronger foes by using keen senses, swift running, and stealth. Their ability to adapt keeps them resilient despite these challenges.

TERRITORY

Coyotes claim territories with scent marking, using urine and scat placed in noticeable spots like trails. They patrol boundary areas and use howling to warn outsiders away. Territories can span from 2 to 30 square miles (5 to 78 square kilometers), depending on food availability. Strong family bonds help defend these spaces and ensure enough resources for their pups.

COEXIST

As coyotes move closer to towns, learning to coexist safely is crucial. Keeping trash sealed, removing outdoor pet food, and fencing yards help reduce conflicts. Recognizing that coyotes control rodent populations shows their valuable place in the environment. By respecting their space and habits, people can live alongside these adaptable creatures with minimal trouble.